**Totally Outrageous Stories!**

**From The Annals of Wild Times**

**By Mark Wilkins**

**Table of Contents**

Outrageous Music Business Marketing Secrets!

Disaster Kills 60,000!

Travel Agent Loses His Head

ISIS Nuclear Plot Revealed!

Cedars Sinus Hospital

Festive Thanksgiving Recipes

Hitler's Image Appears on Dog Crap!

Man Predicts Earthquake!

Synchronized Attacks Cripple The U.S.!

Cause of Global Unrest Discovered!

Basketball Team Owner Given Award

Odd 4th of July Traditions

New Jersey Man Talks to God

The Day The Music Died

Horror Movie Review

Is Your Boyfriend is too Kid Friendly?

Vladi Sings The Hits!

A New Study on Discord in America

A Fake Citation

An Ode to Shakespeare

A New Species Discovered

A Controversial Executive Order

Controversial New Reality TV Show

New Fashion Trend Sweeps Europe!

Crappy Homes

Controversial New TV Show on OTN

Murder Most Foul

Contains Outrageous Stories 1, 2 & 3.

Preface

In 1982-83 I created a totally fictitious humor magazine called Wild Times. The stories were fictitious, the Editorial Staff was fictitious and even the writers were fictitious. It featured biting satire that poked fun at literally everybody. No one was safe. Many people were outraged but many others got the humor and thought it was funny as hell. A few years ago, I picked up the banner and began writing new, equally outrageous, stories. They are included in this and future books under the title of Outrageous Stories.

The original Wild Times magazine introduced such characters as The Smoldering Boulders, Dr. Disgusto and The Killer Baby. It invented diseases like Happy Face Syndrome and Chicken Boneheadia. I have some of the items from that magazine in this book but I have also created new material like an ISIS Commander accidentally beheaded by two recruits, and a new disease Cacaworts! Somehow my fictitious disease is now officially listed as a rare disease within the medical community but I assure you, It's totally fictitious. I also introduce some new, colourful, characters like Bill Sutter, Binky Binkleman, Aboo Abu, and Young Adolf's Drawings.

This book is not for the faint of heart or those who are easily offended. It is strictly for college aged and older adults. It is my hope that you "get" the humor in this book and that you enjoy reading it as much as I enjoyed writing it.

P.S. If you can get your hands on an original Wild times Magazine from 1982-83 do so. Besides being as funny as hell, I have seen original copies sell for as high as $82.00 each online.

Sincerely,

M. Wilkins

(and all of the fictitious names used to pen articles in this volume)

## How to get Ahead Dept.

## ISIS Commander Accidentally Beheaded

ISIS Commander Aboo Abu made a big boo boo. He ordered new ISIS Terrorist Recruits Ahmed Ibi and Jamal Washbourg to behead a Christian Militia Leader captured by ISIS in recent fighting. He gave the pair a photo of the leader. They went to the complex where the Militia Leader was held and dragged him out.

When Washbourg excused himself to go to the washroom, Ibi, the lone man guarding the militia leader, was overpowered by him. The Christian Militia Leader ran off. A Frantic Ibi interrupted Washbourg's "alone time". Washbourg rushed out so quickly he left the nude photo of his ISIS Bride 480 pound Uta.

Just as the two men were about to exit the complex they ran into ISIS commander Mustafa Aziz, who, unbeknownst to them looked similar to the Christian Militia Leader because they both had a beard. The two recruits overpowered Aziz, threw a black sack over his head, handcuffed him and took him away to a rock in the middle of the desert. Washbourg pulled out his iphone and shot a video as Ibi removed the black sack, pulled out a machete and began cutting the man's neck.

As he was being cut, the man kept screaming in Arabic "I'm an ISIS Commander you idiots! I'm supposed to do the beheading! You're making abig mistake! No! No! Please don't! It's a Bozo No No! gurgle, gurgle…" Then his head popped off.

Then Washbourg gave the iphone to Ibi as he (Washbourg) walked up to the severed head, grinned, said "Watch this." As he proceeded to kick the severed head 30 yards to his left between two camels. The he shouted "Goal!!!"

The two recruits used their tech savvy skills to upload the video to You Tube on the Official ISIS Propaganda Channel simply called "Death to the Infidel Dogs and Their Muslim Stooges". They titled the video "How to Get Ahead and Make a Goal in The Middle of The Desert". Once it was learned that the two imbeciles actually beheaded an ISIS Commander the video was removed from the ISIS You Tube Channel and put on an ISIS Bloopers and Practical Jokes Channel but it had already gotten 65 million hits before it was removed.

ISIS has put out a fatwa calling for the beheading of its two former recruits who have

been rumored trying to put together funds to
open a Tasty Freeze near Mosul.

---For Wild Times, Itsy Bitsyspider

# The DNC & RNC Announce New Rules for Presidential Debates

Zippy Zipperman, Wild Times Political Correspondent and CEO of Politicon.

Fed up by the tone and nature of the 2016 U.S. Presidential Debates both the Democratic National Committee (DNC), and The Republican National Committee (RNC) have met behind closed doors to devise new Presidential Debate Rules that will insure that an actual debate of the issues occurs.

"The candidates spend more time talking about their opponents character flaws than addressing the issues that the entire Presidential Campaign are supposed to be about." Said Ricardo Rickabono, a prominent member of the RNC Minority Issues Caucus.

"These new rules will insure that an actual debate of the issues breaks out instead of a political gossip fest." Said Madge Plugnutz, DNC Women's Issues Caucus Chair.

Although the rules will not go into effect until the 2020 race, and will not be issued officially until January of that year, our crack team of Wild Times Staffers was able to smuggle a copy from the hands of an angry capuchin monkey whose cage linings come from the DNC. The rules appear below.

DNC + RNC
Official Presidential Debate
Rules

We the DNC & RNC Member, in order to create an atmosphere of authenticity in debate of the political issues that face are nation, do ordain and establish these Presidential debate Rules.

1. At the beginning of each debate, show a black line drawing of each candidate on plain white paper.
2. Every time a candidate goes off topic and begins to talk about their opponent's faults, drown them out by playing circus music,
3. Change camera focus to the line drawing of them and show a hand drawing a colorful clown attribute on the face of their line drawing.
4. Do this every time a candidate goes off topic and hammers their opponent.
5. See which candidate goes "Full Bozo" first.

This should work to force each candidate to spend most, if not all of their time actually debating the issues and explaining their plans for addressing them. Neither candidate would want to be thought of as being a clown, especially if the end result was that they went "Full Bozo". The Rules continue below:

6. Don't show the candidates shaking hands and congratulating each other, at the end of the debate.
7. Instead, close with a shot of the two line drawings side by side so that the American People can see their real choices for President this election cycle.
8. Then play circus music.


  With these rules firmly in place, the next Campaign 2020 s sure to have either lively discussions of real issues of concern or become another circus.

For Wild Times, I'm Zippy Zipperman.

## Give them an inch & They Take A Foot Dept.

## Big Foot Captured!

Weaver Point WA-   In a remote section of forested Washington State Novice Big Foot Hunters Josh Spelling and Bill Sutter made the catch of a lifetime. They captured a living Big Foot!

The pair had spotted a family of bigfoot foraging in the remote area and set a trap for them. The novice hunters set a bigfoot trap by digging a 20 foot deep hole and padding it with a whole bunch of leaves. They covered it with an old bay window frame with cotton mesh. They set 11 similar traps all around the vicinity and checked them regularly.

The pair was surprised when they found a young Bigfoot, approximately seven feet tall at the bottom of one of the holes.

"As we approached the trap we heard a horrible noise, half growl and half scream Said Spelling, "and the smell almost knocked me off of my feet." He continued.

"We checked the trap, and found the little one in it." Said Sutter "Now we just got to figure out how to get him out of the hole." He concluded.
---For Wild Times, I. M. Aconspiracynut

# Presidential Pardon Us Dept.

# The Washington – Lincoln

# Controversy

IN HIS ASTOUNDING NEW BOOK, AUTHOR HANK E. GOO MAKES A STARTLING CLAIM THAT GEORGE WASHINGTON, THE FATHER OF OUR COUNTRY AND ABRAHAM LINCOLN, THE PRESIDENT WHO SAVED OUR UNION WERE ACTUALLY FATHER AND SON! IN THIS WILD TIMES ONLINE EXCLUSIVE, MR. GOO LOOKS AT SOME INCREDIBLE SIMILARITIES BETWEEN THE TWO HISTORICAL FIGURES.

In my studies at The Potato Institute at Screwledge University I came to discover some startling similarities between George Washington and Abraham Lincoln that prove beyond all shadow of a doubt that they are actually father and son! I am certain of this because, such a succession of profound similarities cannot be found between any other

U.S. Presidents. Since both men lived at different times, there is only one possibility to explain these similarities, they are blood relatives! There are three categories of similarities I shall discuss in this scholarly document:

!. Striking Similarities  2. Historical Similarities  3. Recent Similarities

## Striking Similarities:

Washington and Lincoln were both men. They were both U.S. Presidents. They were both born in February. They both had wives whose first name began with the letter "M".

## Historical Similarities:

Lincoln wrote the Gettysburg Address. Washington wrote his address on some stationery!

Lincoln's Vice President had the last name of Johnson. Washington's Vice President was named John and he used to be somebody's son!

Washington died of an allergic reaction to wet clothing and cold weather. Lincoln died of an allergic reaction to a bullet in his head!

Washington died in 1799. Lincoln was born in 1809. **BOTH YEARS END IN A 9 !!!!**

**Recent Similarities: (after 1949 the 150th anniversary of Washington's death)**

Washington was a personal friend of Thomas Jefferson. Lincoln was once mentioned of the T.V. show "The Jeffersons".

Washington had a State named after him. Lincoln had a Continental named after him.

Washington was the name of a character on the TV show "Welcome Back Kotter".

Lincoln was the name of a character on the TV show "The Mod Squad".

Both shows were cancelled years ago!!!

I hope you will join with me in pushing for the Washington – Lincoln Father and Son Memorial Statue. We are just $29,999, 999.88 away from reaching our goal of thirty million dollars. Please contribute. Send your quasi tax free donations to:

Mr. Hank E Goo Retirement in the Bahamas Fund: P.O. Box 111111112, Ripuoff, Illinois 11722

**Fun with Stupid Horror Movies Dept.**

**Plot of the Forthcoming Blockbuster**

**From Dumbass Studios Revealed!**

In a bold move, Wild Times staffers snuck into the offices of Dumbass (pronounced Du Mass) Studios and smuggled the plot of their new action packed horror movie from the writer's mill trashcan. In this Wild Times Exclusive, we give you an insight into one of the best kept secrets in Hollywood!

**The Pickle that ate Kentucky** (plot notes by writer Jaques Tootite)

One day a really dumb brat sprinkled hair growing cream on a pickle in her refrigerator. Then she put it in the microwave with a slice of cherry cheesecake during a lightning storm.

The lightning struck her house, the microwave exploded, out popped the pickle three times its normal size. It also grew arms. Legs and a face. It was a psycho pickle. It started eating everything in her house and as it did it got bigger and bigger and kept on screaming supercalifragilisticexpealidocius!. It was too much of an existential experience for the bratty girl so she ran out of her house to seek refuge in the house of her best friend and neighbor Max. Trying to warn the city of the danger she pasted up posters with a picture of the gigantic pickle and the words Warning if you see this pickle run for your life. Most people thought the girl was being a smartass and ignored the poster so the pickle ate most of the people in the city. The bratty girl feared for her life as the pickle followed her

everywhere eating everyone in its path.
Eventually it choked on a dump truck and
died.

## Trick Or Treat, Smell My Feet Dept.

**Halloween Costumes**

**Gone Berserk!**

Whether you are going to a costume party or looking for just the right costume for your little son or daughter or brother or sister, Wild Times Online has got a costume suggestion to fit any Halloween Occasion. These costume suggestions are not only creative, they are also extremely inexpensive to make and we guarantee, you will be the only one at the party wearing these costumes! Please bear in mind that Wild Times Online, its writers, editors, owners, publishers and staff assume no responsibility for stupidity on the part of the public for anyone that actually does something harmful to themselves or to others or inspires others to harm them or others based on the costumes, directions or anything contained in this article.

1.  Dye your hair green. Coat your skin with thick orange makeup. Wear an orange outfit with horizontal stripes. Go as a carrot.

2.  Wear a black business suit without a tie. Put on a pair of boots. Cover them in cement. Hang seaweed out of your pockets and around your neck. Go as Jimmy Hoffa.

3.  Put a large, brown plastic garbage bag over yourself. Haphazardly glue on a couple of paper legs. Put a dab of red paint here and there. Lay on the floor during the entire course of the party. Don't move. Don't talk. Go as the giant cockroach that was squashed by a freight train.

4.   Put on tight shorts with rips down the sides, a long sleeve shirt two sizes too small and split sneakers. Put lime green makeup on your face, arms and legs. Apply red makeup in small dots all over your face. Put a large cucumber in your shorts. Smear a can of thick, gooey, mushroom soup all over the front of the shorts. Go as The Incredible Hulk at the onset of puberty.

5.   Take a white bed sheet. Pour gasoline over it. Set it on fire. Count to two. Put the fire out. When the sheet cools down, throw it over your head. Cut two eye holes in it. Apply red and black makeup to all areas of your exposed skin. Go as the KKK man who accidentally fell into the burning cross.

6.    Go six days without taking a bath. Put on a brown bathing suit. Smear thick, dark brown makeup all over your body. Go as a tird.

7.    Put on a phony blond handle bar mustache. Shave all the hair off the top of your head. Apply lots of thick red dye and fake blood there. Tape a plastic tomahawk to the top of your head. Put on a Cavalry General's uniform circa 1876. Go as General Custer after Little Big Horn.

**Bonus Halloween Recipe!!!!**

Smashing Pumpkin Pie: Take a 26 pound pumpkin. Go to the roof of a 16 story building. Drop the pumpkin from the roof into a 2 gallon bucket on the sidewalk below. Be sure there are no cars or people below. Serves 3 people.

## Bad Ideas of Olympic Proportion Dept.

The Couch Potato Olympics

In late 2012 a group cult lazy people who thought God was a potato and that the Mayan predictions were about the rise of the couch potato decided to create an epic event that would draw people from all over the world. They got together and decided to create The Couch Potato Olympics. The cult had 63 followers and was based in Idaho.

They spent $165,000 taking ads asking for registrants to pay $100 each to join and represent a nation of their choosing. The first year of the Couch Potato Olympics had only 103 entrants from 3 nations. There were 97 entrants representing the United States, 5 representing Canada and one from the European nation of Moronia who thought he was entering the real Olympics.

From that tiny seed, the Couch Potato Olympics, held on the grounds of Screwledge University have grown each year. The 2016 C.P. Olympics had a whopping 166 contestants representing 14 different nations! Roger Plugnitz is the reigning Decathelete having won that event in 2012, 2014 and 2016. Each year he represents a different nation. In 2016 he represented Zimbabwe just because he liked the way the name rolls off of your tongue.

There are rumors that the 2017 C.P. Olympics will be televised. If you would like to enter as a contestant simply send a $100 bill to C.P. Olympics, Screwledge University, Potato Idaho 12345. Attention: Uncle Bart. Be sure to pick the events you want to enter in and a nation you would like to represent. The events are listed below:

Remote Control Division

Event # 1  Power Lifting
Event #2   Speed Channel Changing
Event # 3  Tossing across the room to another couch

Snacking Division

Event  #1   Power Snacking Chips

Event # 2   Power Snacking Cookies

Event #3   Speed Snacking


Drinking Division


Event  #1   Power Sipping

Event # 2   Speed Guzzling

Event #3   Alcohol Consumption


Bodily Functions


Event  #1   Power Belching

Event # 2   Speed Scratching

Event #3   Speed Bladder Emptying

Decathlon: The cumulative highest score for participants in any 10 different events of their choosing.

## HALF TRUTHS BASED ON REAL EVENTS DEPT.

## MAD DICTATOR EXECUTES MAN

## FOR FALLING ASLEEP

By Sucha Loadacrap

North Korean Dictator Kim Jong Un is at it again. The Minister heading his national defenses fell asleep during a meeting with The Mad Dictator. When Kim tried to wake him up the man dared to talk back to him. So Kim decided to implement the North Korean Retirement Plan. Due to the man's many years of service, Kim decided to give him a really huge sendoff. "He is going to go out with a bang!" said the giddy dictator.

The North Korean Retirement Plan is public execution. Instead of giving the Defense

Minister a simple riflemen execution squad, he put him against a wall and fired anti aircraft guns at him. This was done in front of hundreds of witnesses.

Witness accounts very. Citizen # 7831 said "One second he was there and the next he was smoke and blood splatter."

Citizen # 2394 said "I didn't know Defense Ministers could fly!"

Citizen # 4328 asked Citizen # 8765: "Is the Defense Minister flying today?"

Citizen 8765 replied "I think so."

To which Citizen #4328 responded "You'd better catch him, his nose just flew past my house!"

The execution follows on the heels of 15 other such executions of high ranking officials recently. Kim has executed 70 high ranking officials in all since taking power. He still lags behind Adolf Hitler with 6,898 executions. "I want to go for the record!" he yelled while eating a box of Sugar Frosted Flakes.

Either elements in the leadership of North Korea is not loyal to him, are questioning his authority or he is just plain paranoid. When asked if he might be paranoid the Mad Dictator said "I'm not paranoid, everyone really is out to get me!" he said before laughing hysterically. He then ordered the reporter who asked the question executed by firing squad by Bazooka.

The really scary thing is that this bozo has nuclear bombs and his finger on the nuclear trigger.

## You Call That Art? Dept.

## Lost Hitler Artwork Discovered !

An abandoned mine in near Salzburg Austria has yielded  25 train cars filled with priceless art & antiques stolen by Nazis during World War 2. The train yielded works by Van Gogh, Monet, Rembrandt and the most famous artist of them all Adolf Hitler!

Unbeknownst to many, Hitler began his career as an artist. The Vienna Art Establishment, who were mostly Jewish, rejected his art as amateurish. Hitler himself, thought his art was on the masterpiece level and many of his powerful Nazi friends agreed. During the height of the Third Reich, a Hitler painting could fetch as High as one million Reich Marks.

It is unclear why these exquisite masterpieces by Der Furer were hidden away with the other master works. It is thought that perhaps, the Nazi's knowing that the end of the Third Reich was near, hid these works with the others in an effort to provide proof of Hitler's greatness as an artist.

One can only wonder what would have happened had Hitler's Mastery of art been recognized. Perhaps the world would have gained one great artist and lost a catastrophic World War. Wild Times Staffers smuggled out photographs of the three Hitler artworks along with an in depth analysis of what they are about and why they are great examples of artful genius.

Art piece # 1 is called the olive tree. It is an iconic study of a small home with an olive tree in front of it. The house is simply yet unevenly drawn to represent the simple but crappy style of architecture in the Germany of Hitler's youth. There is smoke coming out of the chimney so, we know that someone is at home. The sun near the middle of the paining shows that it is about 9:45 in the morning which, is the time when Hitler usually had a Bratwurst sandwich. The fact that the branches of the tree appear to form a Teutonic Knight within them lends a touch of surrealism to the painting.

Mutter

Art Piece # 2 is a true masterpiece. In this painting entitled "Mother" Hitler portrays his own, dear mother as a blond haired, blue eyed Goddess in a pink dress. His actual mother was a black haired, swarthy Ug but its his ideal of the perfect German woman and so it is a valid effort. Notice how delicately the dress is blowing in the breeze. The small child in the background is likely Hitler pretending to invade Poland.

Art Piece #3 (The bottom of which was damaged in the war) was entitled Mein Kampf (My Struggle). It depicts a legendary traumatic incident Young Adolf had in his youth concerning dog poop and a new pair of shows. If you compare this painting with photographs of Hitler at the same age you will see that the likeness is stunning. Notice the perfect scale of the hands and feet. Who else could draw such a unique expression on young Adolf's face?

Now these treasures are finally available to be shared with all the world and all the world can judge Hitler, not as a failed megalomaniac with a micro-penis that loved being pooped on, but as a master artist who had talent and beauty to share.

**New Disease Discovered!**

Eleanor Plugrntz was wondering why she had so much pain going to the bathroom. She went to her doctor and was tested for a hernia, hemorrhoid, colon cancer and colitis she didn't have any of them. She was told to change her diet and avoid foods high in fiber. She didn't get better. She lost all hope and resigned herself to living a life full of pain in the bathroom.

Then one day, several months later, she looked down and what she pooped out and saw something funny. Her poop was perfectly circular and looked healthy but here appeared to be a wart on her poop! She called her doctor immediately.

Dr. Galvan Goopa at Screwledge University (Screw U), did extensive tests but couldn't find any cause for the wart. It wasn't until his brother, Dr, gagagoogoo Goopa of the Potato Institute tested the stool sample that the mystery was solved. Dr. Goopa found traces of tissue only found on the inner lining of the colon.

Since he discovered the cause of the malady he got to name it. He resisted the urge to name it after himself, Goopa Poopa and instead went for a logical choice, Cacawort. A cacawort is a wort on the inner lining of someone's colon that gets scraped off during the pooping process and ends up being pooped out.

Dr. Goopa had dreams of discovering a cure that would win him the Nobel Prize in Medicine but since he just discovered a disease and not a cure, he only got the Tidy Bowl Golden Toilet award by the Plumber's Union of Greater Cleveland. So next time you are doing your dooty and see a wart on one, don't panic. You have a cacawort.

## Death and Texas Dept.

## Inventor of "Luke Warm Pockets" Dies

You may not know his name but you are likely familiar with his inventions. Binky Binkleman, the inventor of Luke Warm Pockets, Pop Torts and Chalupa Rolls died of Gasping Hycophytus, a rare lung disorder today.

Binkleman, a cook in a greasy spoon diner in Bull Muffin Texas, experimented with different foods in his off hours. He invented Pop Torts when he stuck a couple of raw tortillas into a toaster. This happened at a time when convenience foods were catching on and Pop Torts was a hit. Luke Warm Pockets were invented sometime later to take advantage of the increased use of microwave ovens.

Binkleman licensed his inventions to various food manufacturers and collected royalties (Luke Warm Pockets to Hustle Foods and Pop Torts to Killog's). Over the years he became a thousandaire off of the royalties. There were of course, some misses along with the hits. Remember Bacon flavored chewing gum and Asparagus ice cream? Those duds are among Binkleman's misses.

So next time you're eating a couple of Luke Warm Pockets remember the Binkster. Having left no family behind, fans of his products are the only ones who will remember him. Binkleman was 86. The fact that he never ate any of the junk food he created is attributed to his longevity.

## ISIS Forces School District to Shut Down

On the evening of Monday, April 1, 2016 several Bored of Education Members for The Los Alamentos Untied School District received an email that caused them to shut down the entire district. They closed all 16 schools, kept all 48 school busses in the motor pool and told the school staffs not to come to work.

At 6:53 in the Morning, Some Oldguy the 87 year old, drunken, Stuporintendent issued a statement to the world that said:

"To everybody in the world. We are under attack! We have received a credible threat. The Boogey Man is coming! ISIS sent us an email! We are closing our schools today. It is better to be safe than sorry. Liquor? I hardly know her!"

Thanks to our extensive contacts in the intelligence community Wild Times has exclusively been able to obtain a copy of the email. It is, as follows:

**DEAR YOU,**

**WE JIHADIS. WE GONNA BLEW YUSE GUYS UP. WE CARRY A BACKPACK AND A JUICEBOX. WE TAKY THE SCHOOL BUS. WE PUT OUR BACKPACKS IN YER SCHOOLS. WE FOLLOWER ALLUH. HALLOWEEN COMING SOON! JIHADI ISLUM 4 EVER. NO JUICE FOR YOU BAD BOY! OKAY, MOM COMING!  GOTTA GO NOW. BYE!  YOU'RE  YOUR FRIEND.**

**ISSI**

Intelligence experts later ruled this email out as a hoax. There were certain telltale signs of tomfoolery, the many misspellings, especially the fact that Islam is misspelled, and Allah is misspelled and begins with a lower case "a". ISIS is also misspelled.

## How To Market Insidious Crap Dept.

## Ideas That Changed the Music Business

The Music business is filled with stories of legendary pioneers who changed the way people record and play music or that change the way the public listens to music. In a time before the concept of "There's no such thing as a bad review" was coined, two music business legends came up with a plan that could be a game changer for not only the music business but for the entire industry of Advertising and the economic destinies of literally every nation on the planet.*

In the 1980's there was a record company that put out releases in several genres but the primary genre they released was punk rock. There was one particular album that focused on themes like the joy of drug addiction and runaways. One particular song, was about a runaway newly arrived in town who was sexually taken advantage of in bus station bathroom. Embedded in the song were random female screams followed by a gravel voiced response of "Welcome to Hollywood!"

The staff at the record company, a middle aged industry pro and an upstart society dropout couldn't figure out how to market this gritty piece of delusional rants set to off key music. They had a big problem because they had already sent copies to stores all over the nation and had to come up with an ad campaign that would get sales moving!

Then the upstart had a crazy idea. Why not position the record into a train wreck! Position it as a record that's so bad it's kind of good. Like something you know is wrong to listen to but you listen to it anyway because you want to see how bad it can actually get! The middle aged industry pro reminded the upstart that no one knew how bad it was because literally no one reviewed or played any of the copies sent out for promotion. The upstart suggested they come up with an ad, consisting entirely of fake bad reviews from around the globe. These are some of the reviews they came up with.

"Oi, I put this crap on my turntable and it literally stopped working WTF!" **---Australian Outback Herald**

"Please to remove this from my country. It is very, very bad karma. Remove it now and never send it here again!" ---The Punjab Review, India

"I No Like It!" **Broken English, the Journal of Patients at the Bedford Mental Institution.**

"Yo puedo esto en mi machina y la cucarachas fue para me casa!"

**---Tijuana Times**

"This is a wonderful record, if by wonderful one means 45 minutes of painful ear torture and nauseating lyrics!" **---Oh Canada! The Journal of the Canadian Association of Patriotic Disc Jockeys**

"Long and lean and tan and lovely the girl from Ipanema play this record and when she does everyone she does say "Es Caca!" ---**Aye Carrumba! Brazil**

"I put your disc on the player. 14,000 fish committed suicide. Please stop making this" **---Raising Salmon for Profit Monthly**

"This offends my nation!" ---**Jacques Tootight, Paris Express**

"This means Jihad, corrupt Western Dogs!" ---**Terrorist Camp News, Syria**

"Who maky poo poo on song?" ---**Little Marvin, McMartin Pre-School Review**

"I try eat. No me like. Too much chewy. I like banana! I No like black round thing. Next time, send banana!" ------**Tarzan, Jungle News**

"Imperialist Yankee Garbage!" ----**Shanghai Sentinel, People's Republic of China**

"Seriously? You send us this? You People suck!" ---**What's On, London**

This disc is  smash! I smash it in my uncle Bucaki's ugly face! Nyet, Nyet. No Good!  -----**Painsky! The Journal of the Russian Communist Torturers Union.**

The entire ad campaign raised national sales of the record from 13 to 21 units. The ads did however, amuse the thousands of people who saw them. That amusement however didn't translate into sales. The Record Label survived this disaster but the recording artists who made the record couldn't find another company to finance any future recordings.

*It could have been if it were successful. It was, in fact an abysmal failure.

----Snooty Snootington, on Assignment for Wild Times

## Disaster Films We'd Like To see Dept.

Ever wonder what would happen if a low budget, company had a reporter that was obsessive compulsive as the first on the scene of a major disaster. It would look something like this.

Giant Disaster Kills 60,000 helpless people!

A Giant Disaster Killed 60,000 helpless people! The day began just as many others do. It was a peaceful day. People rising and getting ready for work. Children going off to school.

Then suddenly, The earth began to shake! Then, hurricane force winds kicked in! As the ground continued to shake, buildings collapsed! Gas mains and gas stations blew up! Fires raged everywhere! Men used to telling their wives "Don't get your panties in a bunch." Couldn't, because their wives panties were all burnt up!

People already out on the streets ran for their lives! Well, some actually drove. Technically, some also rode bicycles, or skateboards or wheel chairs. People inside who weren't crushed or burnt, curled up into a ball and cried! "Boo Hoo! Boo Hoo!" Within an hour, 80% of all the buildings collapsed. 26,000 people lay dead. Well, technically they didn't all lay dead some were buried in rubble in an upright or sideways position.

One reporter at the scene eloquently described it in four words. He said "The Horror, The Horror!" well, actually it's two words repeated not four words, but I digress. Screams, sirens and jackhammers were all that could be heard. One little girl was crying "Where's my stuffed bear Mr. Fluffy! The stench of death and moldy concrete filled the air. The scene was total devastation. The fortunes lost. The loved ones lost.
Poor Mr. Fluffy! The agony of nature's fury. Played out as a tragedy of epic proportions. Then the dam broke! This happened today at.... Oh, sorry, we ran out of film!

## How to Get Ahead Dept.

## The Travel Agent Loses His Head

In January 2012 two wanna be movie stars were walking their dog in Griffith Park in Hollywood California. As they neared the famed Hollywood sign, their dog picked up a plastic bag, shook it repeatedly, something the dog did often. The ladies were shocked and grossed out when a severed human head fell out of the bag.

"Our dog Mushy always shakes random bags he finds but usually all that falls out is garbage and used condoms" Said Fluffy McFeely, one of the two aspiring starlets.

" I don't know what to say but please print this because I want my 15 minutes of fame too."

said her walking partner and fellow "actress" Goofa McGurgle

"I've heard a lot of stories about people trying to get ahead in Hollywood but this one is a first!" Said Officer Beatemgood, a random cop who was on the scene when our crack team of reporters arrived.

Soon over 100 police officers and fire fighters were on the scene searching for a body. They found two severed feet and two severed hands. When they put them together with the head, they thought someone had murdered Mr. Potato Head but soon realized that there were no APB's on Mr. Potato Head.

Lab identification yielded that the head belonged to a man who was a retired airline ticket agent. His live in boyfriend had reported him missing the day before . The boyfriend became the center of the investigation when it was discovered that the body had been dead for a couple of weeks and he was only reported missing the day before the head was found.

The boyfriend was recently arrested for the murder.  He was arrested in San Antonio Texas where he had moved shortly after the head was discovered. The trial is due to begin in the near future. They City of Los Angeles is waiting for the next fiscal year to kick in so they can afford the cost of the suspect and a Texas Ranger to accompany him on a Greyhound bus from San Antonio.

<u>**Stupid Pet Tricks Dept.**</u>

**Belgian Raid Reveals an ISIS Nuclear Plot**

BRUSSELS---Belgian authorities found evidence of an ISIS nuclear plot among the documents and items recovered in recent raids in Brussels . Besides the usual guns, computers and animal porn, was evidence of a bizarre plot to use insects to carry miniature dirty bombs. An ISIS Pamphlet entitled "Cockroach Breeding for Fun and Profit", contained all kinds of encrypted information about using tweezers to stuff nuclear material into miniature backpacks, strapping them onto the backs of trained cockroaches and sending them out to specific targets before then detonating them all simultaneously with a single detonator.

Belgian encryption expert Iva Gotnoclue stated "We are surprised how easily we were able to decipher their sophisticated encryption with the help of a decoder ring we got in a box of cereal."

The pamphlet went onto to explain the program which includes an aggressive cockroach breeding program in Mosul with a genetic engineering component, guidelines for romance and breeding, training tactics and cockroach dietary restrictions. The most interesting section discussed the pros and cons of beheading cockroaches who did not obey orders.

Authorities converged upon a roach infested, run down apartment building and found the pamphlets, evidence of a tiny obstacle course, a very small amount of bomb making material and approximately 100 tiny backpacks. Unsure which cockroaches were members of ISIS and which were not, authorities had to exterminate them all.

Colonel Jacques Tootite of the Belgian Secret Service stated "Strike another blow against ISIS and a goal for the Belgian National Team." He stated proudly. "We are thankful we caught this plot before the next generation was hatched." He added.

ISIS Spokesman Idi Ot denounced the concept of a Cockroach Nuclear Program. "Why would we misuse such a valuable source of food?" He asked.

For Further Information dial 411.

At Cedars Sinus Hospital we really care about your bottom, not the bottom line. In fact if you need a proctologist we've got one that will fit…your budget that is! Whether you have facial ringworm or suffer from the heartbreak of Psoriasis our competent staff can assist you. If you like doctors with poofy hair and halitosis schedule an appointment with one of our Poofy Haired doctors today. If you are the victim of motocross accident, are incontinent or are just plain stupid, we can help. Even if you can't normally afford a Podiatrist our Podiatrist can affordably stop the Flesh Eating Bacteria from devouring your big toe. And if you are traumatized by your pig nose, our plastic surgery department can make a silk purse out of your sow's ear. We have the finest surgical team money can buy and even though our chief surgeon is named Dr. Bozo, there are no clowns here. So next time you get sick, go to Cedars Sinus Hospital quick. Cedars Sinus, medical minds solving medical problems with a Bozo at the Helm.

**Food and other disgusting things Dept**.

**Festive Thanksgiving Recipes**

By Dr. Disgusto

I have tried to plan a complete and nutritious thanksgiving feast for you including an entree. Side dish and desert. I hope you people appreciate all of the time and effort I put into planning this meal for you.

**Stuffed Turkey Surprise (Shake & Bake Turkey)**

Take a ten pound turkey. Pull its bowels out. Stick a faucet up its butt and rinse it out real good. Then stuff it full of diced onions, sliced mushrooms, strained carrot baby food (any brand), and one large bag of potato chips.

Tie the sucker's legs together. Raise it up over your head and shake it long enough to give the baby food a chance to coat the potato chips (usually about six or seven minutes). It helps to relieve the monotony if you jump around to your favorite danceable song, like Get On Her Good Side, by Evan Lee Lovefire, for example: https://www.youtube.com/watch?v=lJYJ1KkET5E while you are jumping around shaking the turkey over your head. Make sure the legs are tied together though, or the baby food will dribble all over your forehead.

Once the shaking is over, put the turkey into an oven and bake at 350 degrees until golden brown or until the potato chips burn to a stink.

**Serves 67**

**Special Cranberry Sauce.**

Go to the market and buy a can of slim price cranberry sauce. Put it in the refrigerator for two days. On the day of the big event, open the can and put the contents into a nice serving bowl. Tell everyone you made it yourself.

**Serves 12**

**Cool Whip Crunch**

Take 16 one pound tubs of Cool Whip. Pour them into the bathroom sink. Rev up the egg beater. Put the cool whip with one hand while pouring the contents of a two pound bag of birdseed with the other. Scoop up whatever is left in the sink and put it into bowls.

**Serves 3**

<u>**Crapping on Adolph Dept.**</u>

**Hitler's Image Appears**

**on a Piece of Dog Crap!**

Denver Colorado---In the U.S. State where German Adolph Coors began brewing beer decades ago a miracle of sorts has occurred. There have been many news stories in the past about an Image of The Virgin Mary appearing on a wall or an image of Jesus appearing on a tortilla but just at the time that the Adolf Hipster movement is in full bloom, an image of Der Furher himself came blooming out of a dog's rectum.

Mrs. Helda Weinerschnitzel was walking her dog fluffy when he stopped to go poo all over her neighbor, Mrs. Howell's, lawn. Mrs. Howell began yelling at her to clean up the mess. When Helda looked down at the poop she saw it. It was a perfect likeness of Adolph Hitler looking up at her. 94 year old Helda was a member of the Nazi party when Hitler ruled Germany, so, instead of cleaning it up, she carefully put it on a piece of plaster and called her local chapter of United Racists.

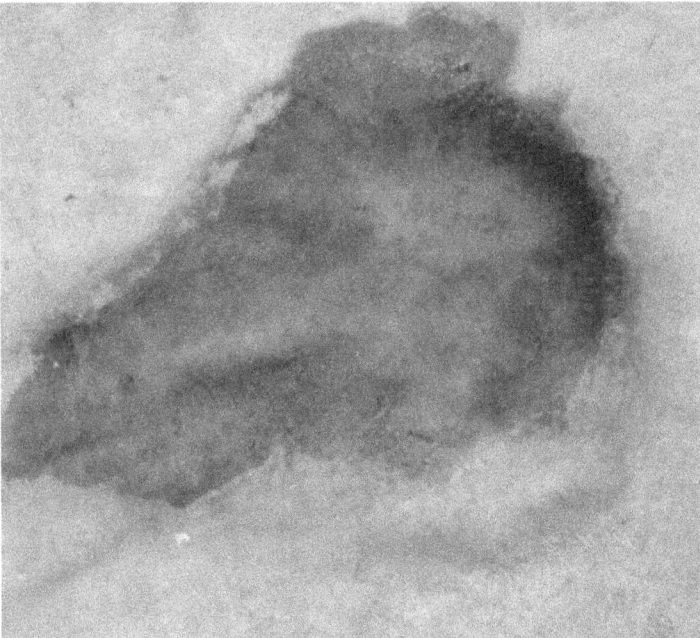

*Looking at the righthand side of the tird one can clearly see*

*Der Fuhrer staring back at you.*

Within minutes, Racists from all over the southwest began lining up to see their hero's image on a piece of poop. There was so much traffic at her house she so beer, bratwurst and pretzels to the people in line. After three hours, she began charging $3.00 admission. She made over $1,000 on the first day.

"This is wonderful!" Said Harry Hess a white supremacist from Mississippi. "I went through the line three times because I just couldn't believe my eyes!"

On the second day, thousands of offers came in regarding the miraculous piece of poop. Some of the more interesting were KKK Grand Wizard Ima Dumshit offered $3,500 for it. A woman who called herself Donna Trump offered highly coveted tickets to The Republican National Convention. She was ruled out as a fake however when, as proof of ownership of the tickets she sent in a Xerox of a pair bozo lookalike contest tickets. A man named Arnold Shicklegruber sent a legal notice claiming the poop because he owned the rights to all likenesses of Hitler (whose real last name was Schiklegruber).

There was even an offer from ISIS. The Sockacaca branch of ISIS offered to decapitate the image of the head from the poop. ISIS Spokesperson Idi Ot issued a press release regarding the matter. Excerpts of it appear below.

Dear Infidels! We of ISIS admire the work of Mr. Hitler very much, we will have to decapitate him from his poop because he is an infidel. We have sent a squad of dedicated Jihadists to steal him right from under the noses of America. Unfortunately when we told them to go to North Colorado, they went to North Carolina instead and mounted an assault on a Der Weinerschnitzel. Though they fought bravely, our five member squad had their plans foiled by the manager who repeatedly hit them in their heads with a corn cob."

After much bickering and interest the winning bid of $10,000 went to the International Racist Museum next to the State Capital building in Arizona.

"I chose them for three reasons." Said Weinerschnitzel "they offered the most money, more people would be able to see it and they would have the expertise to preserve the holy relic as it was beginning to get a bit runny.

In a surprising turn of events, just as museum staff were about to take the valuable artifact away, a member of the Jewish Defense League through some gasoline on it and set it on fire. When someone yelled fire, a white supremacist from Kentucky stomped on it trying to put the fire out. Museum Staff are trying to see if they can reconstruct the image by peeling feces off the bottom of the supremacists boot.

We tried to contact Adolph Hitler's publicist Joseph Goebbels for a comment but he has been dead for over 75 years.

## Disastrous Moments in History Dept.

## Man Predicted massive earthquake would
## Hit California on Friday May 29, 2015!

"Psychic" Samuel San Andreas made a viral video on You Tube. The video predicted a massive 8.8 earthquake would hit California sometime on May 29, 2015.

The video was filmed in a darkened bath room lit by the light of one lone candle. On the mirror are the words We're all Going ta Die, in smeared red lipstick. A bald man in a moo moo and black eyeliner appears. He is shaking. His eyes begin rolling. He says "On May 29th 2015 there will be a massive 8.8 level earthquake!" in a deep voice that sounds like it came from the depths of hell. Then he sneezes and blows out the candle. Then a sobbing voice whispers "The Rock is our only salvation…" the video stops there.

The video was made on May 28, 2015 and went "viral" garnering 13 hits in 16 hours.

When Officials from the California seismological Institute were asked about the possibility of the prediction coming true they had no comment.

In an unrelated story, the film San Andreas, a fictional drama about an 8.8 earthquake hit theaters throughout California on May 29, 2015.

---B.S. Youtuby

## Stinking Govt. Dept.

## Synchronized Attacks Cripple U.S.

By Jay L. Bate

Breaking News- 27 Major cities in the U.S. were hit by a synchronized Terrorist attack today when an unknown Terrorist group exploded bombs at sewage treatment plants. New York, Chicago, Los Angeles, Washington D.C., Boston, Atlanta, Dallas, Omaha, Minneapolis, Seattle, Phoenix, Philadelphia, Cleveland, Detroit, Indianapolis and Milwaukee were among the cities hardest hit.

In a press release the White House declared this to be "The biggest attack against America has seen in since the fall of the stock market several years ago."

The infrastructure of all of the cities affected is heavily affected as the various cities scramble to rebuild sewage treatment plants. Many are diverting raw sewage to nearby rivers and oceans. Phoenix hired 70,000 ditch diggers and dug a ditch that reaches the Grand Canyon.

"Our city doesn't have a nearby body of water and we are concerned about the public health and safety of our townspeople." Said Mayor Aye Dontcareaboutyou in a lame attempt to justify trashing a national monument. "With the depth of the Grand Canyon we won't have to worry about rebuilding our sewage treatment plant for years." He continued.

When asked about his reaction to the attack, Homeland Security Chief Maclemore

McHamburgler said "I smell a rat." On his way into a Cabinet meeting.

When asked for his opinion, infamous Russian Spy Ima Pootin' declared "I always knew America was full of crap, I guess now they will find out how much crap they are full of."

## Scientists Discover The Root Cause of Global Unrest

When you ask most people about what the root cause of global unrest, some will say it is greed. Others will say it's a clash of cultures. Still, others will say it is prejudice.    Could it be something else? Could it be something so simple that it has flown below the radar for centuries?

Researchers at The New Institute of Analytical Pharmacology at Screwledge University, have discovered the root cause of global unrest. "Homophones are the cause of many of society's problems because homophones insidiously thwart attempts at communication and muddle up the meanings of words, phrases and sentences." Said Harry Balls, spokesperson for the Institute.

Balls went onto explain that the use of homophones is common in communications in all languages around the globe. He illuminated us with the fact that, contrary to popular belief, homophones are not telephones set aside for exclusive use by a particular percentage of the population but words that sound like other words that are spelled differently and have different meanings.

"It begins with simple interpersonal communications and ends with international misunderstandings and even, in some cases, wars between nations." Balls continued.

Sometimes it is a word in a sentence and other times it is someone's birth name. Balls went onto give the personal example regarding a friend of his. It is well known that Harry Balls is close friends with Austrian Rocket Scientist Fa Cueall. Cueall has no problems in her native Austria where Fa is a very common first name. In fact, it ranks fourth in popularity behind Doe, Ray and Mi and ranks just above So, La, Ti and Dough. This is due to the Von Trapp Syndrome that runs rampant throughout the suburbs.

When Ms. Cueall comes to The U.S. however, she has a myriad of problems. She has been held at the airport by U.S. Customs Officials several times because they seriously question the authenticity of her passport. She has also been hauled into the police station several times because local policing authorities don't believe her New York State Driver's License is real. Fa Cueall points out that problems of this nature are not the exclusive domain of people whose names are homophones; it also applies to people who have the same name as celebrities. She related a similar incident that happened to her fiancée who happens to have the unfortunate name of Mickey Mouse.

So next time you think someone is making fun of you, check and see if they aren't merely using a homophone. Chances are you will stop a fight before it begins and strike a blow against misunderstanding. Not Miss Understanding, my former second grade teacher but misunderstanding, thinking someone is saying something when they are not. --For Wild Times, Ling Wistic

## Sounds So Real Its Gottabe Fake Dept.

**NAACP Cancels Clapper Owner's Lifetime Achievement Award,**

**KKK Offers Him One Instead**

By Jerry "Beave" Nathers

The NAACP announced today that it has cancelled Los Angeles Clappers owner Ronald Studling's Lifetime Achievement Award. It did so, citing racist comments allegedly made by Studling on a tape authored by an ex-girlfriend that his family is suing for embezzlement. The girlfriend served under Studling in a position with the Clappers front office.

News of the cancelled award prompted Ima Crackhead, Grand High Mucky Muck of the Ku Klux Klan to issue a press release stating that they were willing to give Mr. Studley the highest award the "organization" gives non-members, the coveted "Champion of Racism" award.

Mr. Studling refused to comment when a Wild Times correspondent tracked him down at a KFC.

<u>**Crapping on a Holiday Dept.**</u>

**Odd 4th of July Traditions**

Most people celebrate the 4th of July by having a picnic and watching fireworks. That is not how it has always been. That is not how it is always celebrated.

In the early days of our nation people celebrated with bonfires. In Salem Massachusetts they burned witches in the bonfire. In New Orleans they burned Gumbo. In Jamaica Queens they burned Marijuana. That particular tradition has spread nationwide and lasts the whole year long.

In the early 1800's patriots would dress like their favorite founding father and walk around greeting people. This tradition was especially popular at mental institutions. After the civil war, in some areas of the south they held a redneck rally where they put out confederate flags, drank beer, watched car races and married their cousins.

In the 1960's hippies celebrated Independence Day by protesting the Vietnam War and shooting off fireworks towards the ground. The most famous person to do this was Jack Flash who was known as Jumping Jack Flash because he had to jump around to dodge the fireworks headed towards his feet. One of The Rolling Stones read a newspaper article about him one 4th of July and penned their hit Jumping Jack Flash. Jack Flash was also credited with inventing a popular dance. When a firework nipped his left foot one 4th of July, he started dancing around in agony. TV news cameras captured the event and the

"Hot Potato" dance craze erupted across America.

So eat your hot dogs and apple pie but while you are having fun, remember that the 4th of July hasn't always been that way. Just like the diversity of the American population, there is diversity in the way Americans have and do celebrate their independence.

---For Wild Times, Weezer Jr.

## Holy Dumbass Dept.

## New Jersey Man Claims to Talk to God

Crackpot New Jersey- Bruno Zepete is a mild mannered plumber who shocked neighbors recently when he told them that he talks to God. He never told them what God said to him only that he talked to God. Deeply religious people began to camp out, outside of his modest one bedroom house, waiting for him to reveal what God told him. Whenever he went out of his house, to work on a job or to shop for groceries, people would follow him and ask what God told him.

The crowd around Zepte's home grew so large that it impeded the flow of traffic. Local police were assigned to the area to keep campers off of city streets. Local news reporters began to show up but Zepete refused to give any of them an interview.

After one month passed, Zepete agreed to give an interview to Fox News for an undisclosed sum of money. Two minutes into the interview, Zepete's story unraveled, people who were camping out at his house left and he was met with scorn whenever he left his house.

Soon after the interview began, the reporter asked how God contacted him Zepete said "God called me on the phone." When the reporter asked what God Told him, Zepete replied "God told me to buy penny stocks, then, as if ordained by God, one minute later, I got a phone call from a guy selling penny stocks." I knew God had sent him, because he sounded just like God."

"I'll bet that was the last you heard from God" said the reporter.

"Actually no," replied Zepete, "I got a call from God a week later but this time he told me to buy office supplies." He continued.

"I'll bet you didn't buy the office supplies".
Said the reporter.

"Of course not!" stated Zepete emphatically, "I told God I lost my entire life savings when the penny stock market crashed a couple of days after I got the first phone call."
===Ima Profit

## The Day The Music Died

If you've ever heard of disco music or funk music it is likely because of him. Famed Songwriter and Bass player Ebola "Bones" Jones died tragically. Jones went missing about a month ago when he was in the middle of a comeback tour. His body was found in the middle of an Iowa cornfield.

Jones got a reputation as a bad ass bass player when doing sessions for such R&B bands as The Tentations, The Bur Kays, and The Gape Band. He developed a hybrid style of bass playing and music that was a fusion of disco and funk called Disfunktion.

The colorful and controversial songwriter penned a lot of hit tunes but the two he will be most remembered for are " The Corn Song" and "America The Bootyful" both of which caused a lot of controversy and made headlines but yielded lackluster sales.

"America The Bootyful" was Jones attempt to replace the unofficial national anthem "America The Beautiful" with his own hybrid version. A comparison of some of the lyrics from each song will illustrate why his version never caught on.

From America The Beautiful: "Oh beautiful for spacious skies for amber waves of grain, for purple mountains majesty above the fruited plain."

From Jones version: "Oh bootyful for spacious cracks for ample waves of fat, for purple panties dangling, above the booty plane."

Jones didn't do himself any favors by suing the U.S. Government for racism for not adapting his anthem. The case was dismissed by Superior Court Judge Anthony Weener as "frivolous and a colossal waste of time."

Jones other controversial song was "The Corn Song" which he promoted as "replacing" the classic "Happy Birthday to You". With lines like "Happy, happy birthday, I'm sorry you were born, instead of getting presents, I hope that you get corn!" It's not hard to understand why it didn't catch on. It did however start a trend of sorts. It started the trend of giving corn to people you don't like on their birthday, celebrated by literally dozens of people across America.

Ironically, Jones bones were found in the middle of the corn field, face down in the opening of a giant ant hill in the shape of a booty. It is surmised that he got drunk and couldn't find his way out of the cornfield and fell into the ant hill. No funeral plans have been announced.

-----For Wild Times, Rock M. Sockem

# Wild Times Movie Review Dept.

# The Pickle That Ate Kentucky

The movie "The Pickle That Ate Kentucky" was a very strange movie. The setting of the movie is in modern day Kentucky. The Plot involves a mad scientist that brings a gigantic pickle to life. The pickle grows arms, legs, and a face. It gets hungry and starts eating everything in sight. As it eats it gets bigger and bigger. The characters include Bozono (the mad scientist), the pickle, various people who get eaten or try to kill the pickle and Sparky the wonder pig.

Different characters compete to see who can kill the pickle. The pickle begins to worry when he suffers separation from the mad scientist. Various Crips and Bloods represent for their hood but all of them get eaten by the big pickle. A funny scene happens when the pickle eats all the people at the State Academic Decathlon in the middle of the championship round. As the pickle eats more and more it becomes a real heavyweight and finally dies of exhaustion from eating so much. We give the movie 3 out of five fingers.

---Lou Serofalltime

# Top 10 Warning Signs That Your Boyfriend is a Little Too Kid Friendly

1. Chuck E Cheese has a restraining order against him

2. He keeps leaving his business cards in sandboxes.

3. His mini-van looks suspiciously similar to an ice cream truck.

4. He has every season of Romper Room on Blu-Ray.

5. There is an FBI Most Wanted Poster of him at the Kiddyland Post Office.

6. He goes on vacation to The Children's Zoo every year.

7. He shows up to your nieces sweet 16 party wearing X-Ray glasses.

8. He has a Platinum Credit card with Toys R Us.

9. His car radio is tuned to radio Disney.

10. He can sing every Wiggles song from memory.

## Fun with Dictators Dept.
## Vladi Sings The Hits

After the Death of Rock Icon Fats Domino a tape of Russian President Vladimir Putin singing "Blue Berry Hill" in Karoake surfaced. Seizing upon the moment Jackoffsky Pumperdinkynyet Owner of Kremlin Karaoke collected a mini CD's worth of secret recordings he made of Putin singing other iconic songs. He sold it to us and now we are releasing the mini CD for you, the fans. In this CD Mr. Putin demonstrates that he is not only a fantastic singer but quite an astute songsmith as well. Here is an example of some of the lyric rewrites of the songs on the CD!

**Blueberry Hill by Fats Domino**
I found my thrill
On blueberry Hill
When I found my capitalist oppressor
And then I shot him in the head
Bang!

**Cell Phone by Drake**
You don't call me on the cell phone
After I put you in the cell block
You don't call me on the cell phone
Because there's no reception in the gulag!

**Hello by Adele**
Hello from the other side!
I waited til you opened wide
Then I poured in the poison
It ate up your heart
Now Boris is chopping up
The rest of your parts

**Stairway to Heaven**
And there's a President we all know
And he is very sure
He's going to stay in power now
And in the future he'll be there
To lead our nation out of despair
and he's buying the stairway to
The Kremlin!

**Hotel California**
**Verse**
On a dark Ukraine highway
Cold wind in my hairs

Warm smell of victory
And a warm port in wintair
**Chorus**
Welcome to the Warm Port l Crimea
What a lovely place
Now we own this space
We're living it up at the warm port Crimea
If you come next year
We will still be here.

Yes! Now you can experience the true genius
of Vladimir Putin in this internet exclusive
offer called: Vladi Sings The Hits! You get: a
five song mini CD and lyric sheets so you can
sing along with the King of Kremlin Karaoke!
Rush $6.95 to: Vladi Sings The Hits! P.O. Box
918176, Crackpot KY, 012345. Wait six weeks
for delivery. If you still don't get it send
another $6.95 to the same address. Keep on
sending the money every six weeks until your
CD arrives.

## Pointless Studies Dept.
## New Study Shows Why There is Discord in America!

A new study shows that people that drive a GM trucks will not do business with people who drive Ford trucks! The study by the Business Survey School at the Potato Institute at Screwledge University compared results from 13,000 truck owners who also owned their own businesses. The respondents owned 435 different businesses in various business categories. The businesses ranged from internet to brick and mortar and included retail, wholesale, and service businesses. The respondents lived in lived in 43 different American states.

"It was a surprise to us!" Stated Dr. Friederich Asslips , the professor who developed the survey. "We actually thought that they would be willing to do business with each other based on the fact that they are just good Americans but we found that there is actually a lot of animosity because they are just backward rednecks!"

Clem Inbread, a spokesperson for the Backwards Rednecks Association of America "We believe this study is hog slop. Besides, how can you trust any study by a Doctor whose name is Ass lips?

## Pissing Off Motorists Dept.
## A Fake Citation

Have you ever been the victim of someone who parks their car inappropriately? Copy this citation and put it on their window!

### Parking Enforcement Citation

This citation has been issued to you for parking like a drunken donkey. How can someone who does such a crappy job parking have gotten a license? Next time you park like this the parking fairy is going to pour sugar into your gas tank and let the air out of one or more of your tires, you inconsiderate lump of brain pudding!

**An Ode to Shakespeare**

William Shakespeare was perhaps the greatest author in the history of the English Language. His literary works have shaped how the English speaking world speaks and thinks. His works have influenced books, and even films. Every year on Shakespeare's birthday, People all over the world memorize and speak one of his famous sonnets. Most people pick something from Romeo and Juliet or Richard the Third. Real scholars of the Bard recite one of his lesser known works. Which, unknown to most, have still played a role in shaping how society uses language. Here now are some of his lesser known sonnets.

"There I sat,
Upon my thrown
Broken hearted

Verily I cometh to poop
But alas, only farted."
*From: Act 2 Scene 3, Richard the Turd*

"A cursed pox upon my bowels did rage!
For a fortnight I cried out in pain!
But forsooth, I heard the sweet sound
Of the elixir that would be my sole salvation...
Plop, plop, fizz, fizz!
*From: Act 1 Scene 4, The Alka of Seltzer*

"A birdy, a sweet, beautiful birdy
In flight upon the crimson sky
Dropeth a tirdy upon my eye
I donteth careth Birdy bye
For I am joyful
That oxen cannot fly!"
*From: Act 1 Scene 1 Romeo & Pooeyelet (the
prequel to Romeo and Juliet*

"The thatched roof,
"The thatched roof,
The thatched roof has a fire upon it!

We, therefore need no water,
Let that cuckold burn!
Burn, Cuckold, Burn!"
*Act 1 Scene 2 Roasting King John*

'There once was a wench from Nantucket...."
*From A Mid-Summer Night's Dream*

## Warped Science Dept.
## New Species Discovered!

Intrepid Explorer Tyler Whoopendale was trekking through the Amazon Rainforest in Brazil when something interesting caught his eye. He saw a group of spiders attacking a small mouse. The brown, hairy spiders with clown like faces were repeatedly sinking their fangs into the poor animal's stomach. Within a minute, the animal was dead.

Then, the spiders did something very odd. They danced around and had spider sex on the carcass. Then the female spiders crawled into the ears and open mouth of the mouse and laid eggs. Whoopendale went back to the site for the next 8 days and noticed the degeneration of the carcass. He noticed flies laying their larva in the bloated body. He noticed baby spiders hatching and then maggots hatching. The maggots provided the baby spiders with a food source.

Whoopendale didn't realize it until he got back to civilization but he had discovered a new species of spider! As is custom with scientific discoveries, the scientist who makes the discovery has the naming rights to it. Whoopendale resisted his egocentric urge to name it after himself. He rejected names like the Whoopendale Brown Spider or the Whoopendale Clown Face. He also resisted corporate attempts to name it. He didn't like the idea of calling it something like the Diet Pepsi Spider or the  Mitsubishi Brown Spider. In the end, he chose to name it after the gulch nearest the place where he forest saw the spider.  So open up the encyclopedias, people of the world, say hello to the Ichigoochimama Spider.

Species : Anthropoda
Class: Arachnida
Order: Araneae
Family: **Theraphosidae**
Name: Ichigoochimama

Habitat: Brazilian Rain Forrest

Description: Averaging a quarter of an inch in length,  brown, hairy with clown like faces. Habits: These spiders hunt in packs, sting small mammals to death and then lay their larva in the carcass to feast off of maggots and other vermin feasting on the carcass as it degenerates.

**Executive Disorder Dept.**
**Controversial New Trump Administration Executive Order**

The Trump Administration's new Executive Order "A Day without Cell Phones" takes a bold step towards solving a problem that has long been ignored by government. The order would pick a random day and call it "A Day without Cell Phones". Anyone caught using a cell phone on that day would be given a $10,000 fine.

The Federal Government will text every cell phone customer in America the day before to let them know when it will be. When reporters asked what would happen to those who didn't get the text, Officials in the Justice Department said that the just sending the text constituted fair warning under federal civil rights statutes and that no excuses for cell phone use would be accepted. To insure accuracy of the data, the NSA is supplying all of the cell phone numbers that will enable the government to do this. The information was further verified through the Hackers Bureau at the Russian Embassy.

An unnamed White House Spokesperson stated that the Executive Order was written to help bring attention to the rampant cell phone addiction among U.S. Citizens. He further commented that cell phone use does more than cause car, bus, plane and train accidents, overuse has been known to cause cancer and brain rot, a fungal disease caused by electromagnetic stimulation of brain juices. The disease, though rare, is more prevalent in users who hold cell phones next to their ears for long periods of time.

## Unreal TV Dept.
## Controversial New Reality TV Show Debuts on CMT!

A controversial new reality TV show debuts tonight on Country Music Television (CMT). The show, entitled "Hillbilly Hookups" revolves around upscale urban hipsters and retirees joining an online dating service called "Photodate". The dating service features 10,000 photos of singles aged 18-95. The unique factor is that there is not information on any of the people in the photos. Clients simply scroll through photos and pick the photos of the people they are attracted to.

The photos clients select are then ranked by the client in order of preference and put into their folder. A Photodate facilitator then calls the various people selected by the client and arranges for them to meet for coffee and discover one another. What the clients do not know is that virtually all of the 10,000 prospective "dates" are actually hillbillies whose features were glamourized and photo shopped to make them all look like executives, heiresses and tycoons. The first face to face encounters are then filmed.

Hilarity ensues when unsuspecting hipsters meet the backward, uneducated and often toothless hillbillies. Biff, a 41 year old corporate executive for a Fortune 500 company thought he was going on a date with a 30 something, thin heiress to a catsup fortune almost had a heart attack when he met his actual date, a 56 year old 400 pound, grey haired woman who works at a catsup factory. When asked where the woman in the photo was, the woman simply replied "She got married, had five kids, divorced and ate a whole lotta donuts in the 20 years since the photo was taken. When asked why she would lie about herself like that she replied "Who the hell would go out with someone who looked like me except Floyd the 98 year old blind guy who works cleaning toilets at the Walmart."

Controversy erupted when the National Organization for the Preservation of Hillbilly Heritage riled up the entire hillbilly community and asked them to send letters to CMT. Thousands of misspelled, angry letters went to CMT, (Country Music Television) but several thousand others were addressed to Central Mountain Time, Charcot-Marie Tooth disease, Merle Haggard, General Beauregard, Ma and Pa Kettle, Minnie Pearl, Jed Clampett, Colonel Harlan Sanders, Make America Great Again and several dozen cement companies. Most of the letters went unanswered . The show is wedged between two of the networks most popular shows Roadkill Roadshow and The Best of The Grand Ol' Opry Bloopers.

**New Fashion Trend Sweeping Europe!**

A New Trend is sweeping Europe! The Toe Shoe began as a joke from the House of Fartuchi. Renowned Milan Designer Fabio Fartuchi. Himself made one as a gag gift at the engagement party of famous fashion model Cinderella Skinnyminny. Skinnyminny didn't know it was a joke and wore it to the Cannes Film Festival. The Press coverage of the red carpet and she was barefoot, wearing her toe shoe on her left big toe.

## Homebuilder Ads We'd Like To See Dept.
## Crappy Homes

Alexander Crappy has designed affordable homes for over three decades. His experience has taught him one thing: the key to success is giving people what they want. If being able to find a home that is affordable and within your budget is an important factor in your decision to purchase a home, then Alexander has a home built for you.

Many people would like to live in a home built of fine, quality materials, built by skilled craftsmen. They want a home loaded with customized designs and extras. They want to feel like they are coming home to a palace. In short, they want the home of their dreams. Then, they look at the nightmare of what they can afford and realize that their best bet is to buy a Crappy home!

Alexander and his team have spared no time to cut corners and design homes that you can afford today. All of our homes are built of the finest quality wood and stucco that can be purchased at half price. Instead of those expensive double paned windows that insure outside noises cannot enter your sanctuary, a Crappy home provides you with an opportunity to soak in the sights, sounds and smell of your neighborhood by using only single paned recycled glass in our windows. The multiple colors of the recycled glass provide each of our homes with unique windows because no two windows are exactly alike.

Most people would die to get vaulted ceilings and wood floors but a Crappy home includes them at no extra charge! Our vaulted ceilings are all 6 feet from the floor and supported by beams made out of recycled pole vaults. Our entrance doors and all of our floors are made out of recycled pressboard, made from the finest quality sawdust that money can buy! Your friends and family will wonder how you could afford such beautiful entrance doors and flooring. Just don't get them wet or they will turn to a mushy mess that smells strangely enough like a mixture of formaldehyde and cat urine.

Our Roofing and landscaping are unique to each home. Our roofing is steel reinforced (actually steel washed papier Mache) and is guaranteed to last through the wet summer months! Our landscaping uses plants native to the areas where our homes are located. They fit right in with the landscaping of parks, road medians and freeway wilderness patches of their local area, that is, they would be if we didn't dig up the beautiful plants, shrubs and flowers we find in those areas and plant them around our homes.

While most developers take your money and make you wait months or even a full year before your home is built, we can have your home built within 3 days from the time you order it. In fact, industry statistics prove that we have the fastest turnaround time in the industry! Many in the industry wonder how we can make and fulfill such a promise. The secret is in the commitment of our team of skilled craftsman. It's amazing how quickly a home can be built when you give 15 skid row hobos some hammers and nails and a keg of beer!

Our quality standards will keep you up nights but our prices will make you sleep like a baby. When it comes to buying a home, if affordability is your priority, then buy a Crappy Home! If you want a home that is unique and leans a little, buy a Crappy Home! If having money for the little extras in life means more than having little extras in your house, then buy a Crappy Home! If you want a home you can truly afford and don't want to wait to move in, by a Crappy Home! If you have never been able to afford a home before and this is your first home, make it a Crappy Home! When you think AFFORDABLE, Think CRAPPY! Two Bedroom one bath homes start at just $9,363.27. At Crappy Homes we work hard to live up to our name.

And Now For Our Legal Disclaimer:

All Crappy Home prices do not include land. Taxes and governmental fees are not included. Feel free to have any of our Crappy homes inspected by anyone you choose but you pay for the inspection. Crappy Homes is an equal opportunity home seller. We accept cash payments only. No Checks. No credit cards. Crappy Homes is not licensed to business in every state. If you have any questions about whether or not we are licensed to do business in your state call your cell phone number and get a busy signal. Crappy Homes is not associated with The Fly By Night Construction Company, Crappy Penny Stocks, Great Desperations Dating Service, Enemas by Enedina or Alexander's Cemetery Plot Rentals and the fact that we once did business under all of those names is purely coincidental. Crappy Homes is a registered trademark of Alexander Crappy, who himself is a crappy fictional person and registered trademark of Crappy Homes Inc. All sales are final. No refunds or exchanges ever, despite what federal or state laws say. We sincerely hope that you enjoy your new home for many years to come. We also hope for world peace and the end to hunger but we're not expecting those things to happen either. All Crappy Homes, and parts thereof carry a one year guarantee. We guarantee that we will not be in business within one year from the time you purchase your home. Report any and all complaints to The Better Business Bureau, because we are not members and could care less what they think and besides, we like to think of all the fun you'll have when you ask them to look up Crappy Homes.

## Unreal TV Dept.
## Controversial New Show on OTN

A controversial new show on The Outrageous Television Network (OTN) is like a cross between popular reality and game shows like Survivor and The Biggest Loser. Called "Survival of The Fattest", the show focusses on the plight of 25 people weighing between 400 and 600 pounds. Complications quickly arrive during the Welcome All You Can Eat Buffet segment. As producer Marquis De Sade tells it.

"The contestants have been told that they have landed on Cabal Island but during the segment some letters fall off the sign that says Welcome to Cabal Island and the sign then reads Welcome of Cannibal Island" Said De Sade.

A couple of the contestants show some concern but are mostly ignored by the contestants who are busy chowing down. Then, off in the distance, a chanting sound can be heard. It is faint at first but over the course of several minutes, gets louder and louder. The contestants begin to hear what the chant is saying. It's saying "Yummy, Yummy, Yummy, Yummy!"

Soon 300 hungry cannibals show up. Then the chanting stops and in broken English one of them asks "What's for dinner?" The contestants stare at the cannibals with puzzled looks on their faces. One of the contestants begins to speak but before he can get a word out, another cannibal yells "You are!"

The fun ensues when the cannibals chase the contestants around the island. One woman in her 40's couldn't get out of the buffet fast enough and is grabbed by 12 cannibals who begin munching on her thigh. Over the course of the week cannibals search for, capture and eat various contestants. At the end of the week whichever contestants survive participate in a weighoff. Whomever weighs the most can board a helicopter and escape the island. Unfortunately all of the contestants were captured on the first day.

**<u>Murdering True Crime Dept.</u>**
**Murder Most Foul!**

Hollywood CA- Three people were Gruesomely murdered outside of a KFC Sunday Night. The victims all died of suffocation. Each had several pieces of fried chicken jammed down their throats. A crude hand scrawled sign that looked like chicken scratch, was written on a paper shopping bag. It read:

Die cannibal Piggies! Chickens are people too! The Chicken Liberation Front.

A man in a chicken costume with a crushed KFC bucket of chicken in his backpack was arrested in an Arco gas station bathroom three blocks away. The man, "Poultry" Joe Cacadoodle has been arrested for crimes associated with The Chicken Liberation Front, an organization devoted to ending the practice of eating chickens.

"We are familiar with Poultry Joe and look forward to him being cooped up in a jail cell for many years to come." said Officer Bob Beatemgood of the Hollywood Police Department.

# Author Biography

## Mark Wilkins

## A Storyteller

My name is Mark Wilkins. I am best known to my readers as A Storyteller. I pen the A Storyteller Series of Books for Love Force International Publishing. Unlike most other book series, it does not concentrate on a particular character or a particular story line. Instead, it focuses on books of short stories in various genres by a particular author, namely myself. Some of the books in the A Storyteller Book Series include serious fiction (A Week's Worth of Fiction), humorous fiction (Slices of Life) and a mixture of serious and humorous fiction and non-fiction (Classroom Confessions) and supernatural Fiction (Stories of The Supernatural).

The readers who enjoy my books like reading that sparks their imagination. They like stories with memorable and quirky characters on unusual topics. They like unexpected twists and turns in the plot. If any of these things my readers enjoy describe you, then you too will enjoy my writing.

I am comfortable writing in many different genres. I write both humorous and serious fiction. Some of my stories are based on true events, others are totally my invention. It is up to you, the reader, to decide which stores are based on factual events and which are completely my invention because I'm not telling. I like to tell stories and I work very hard at making those stories both compelling and entertaining. I hope you enjoy reading my books.

# Kindle Books by Love Force International Publishing

Whether you are interested in true stories, fiction, humor, action, adventure, spiritual insights, quotes, poetry, self-help or children's books, Love Force International has got you covered. **Our 99 cent commitment,** our commitment to a 99 cent price for all our kindle e book titles so that people around the globe can afford them, means there has never been a better time to stock up on Books published by Love Force International!

**NOTE:** Books with AINs are available now the others will be available soon. All Titles are printed in English. Books with an **SP** after the title also have a version translated into Spanish. A List of Paperbacks will be below, Reader Series books with a paperback version will have **Ppr** on the same line as the title.

**The Reader Series** is a series of readers that are a sampling of writings by one or more authors.

The Prophet of Life Reader (7 Book Sampler) Volumes 1 & 2

What do essays, articles, stories, poetry and quotes have in common? They are all in this sampling of stories, poems and other writings from 7 of The Prophet of Life's writings found in these Kindle books.

**Author:** The Prophet of Life   **ISBN: 978-1-936462-07-0 ASIN: B015D716C0 (Vol 1)   ASIN: B06XBSWKX8 (Vol 2)**

**The Mark Wilkins Reader 7 Book Sampler! Volumes 1 & 2**

One story from seven books by Mark Wilkins. Whether its smart spouses, inquisitive fools, teachers, gangsters or ghosts these books give you a good sampling of stories by the man known throughout the world as A Storyteller.  Within its pages you will find horror, humor and pathos.

 **Author:** Mark Wilkins    **ISBN: 978-1-936462-38-4 ASIN: B01MU0Z51H  Volume 1**

**The Love Force International Reader 7 Book Sampler! 4 Books in This Series**

Whether you want fiction,, humor, children's stories, poetry or quotes these books have got all of those and more! A sampling of 7 different books by three authors offered in Kindle books published by Love Force International.

**Edited by** Evan Lovefire **ISBN:   ASIN: B06XBHD9RX Vol 1, ASIN: B06XBMGLNK Vol 2**

**The Love Force International Sampler, Spanish Books Edition SP Volumes 1 & 2**
These books contain a sampling of 7 different books by three authors translated into Spanish. The books translated include What Faith has Taught me, Controversy, True Stories of Inspiration & General interest and Quotes about God by The Prophet of Life, Stories of The Supernatural, Slices of Life How to Become The Person You've Always Wanted by Mark Wilkins and Classic Children's Stories You've Likely Never Heard, and my first & second books of stupid little fables by Dr. Goose.
**Edited by** C. Gomez **ISBN: ASIN:** B06XB3RJ2K
**Vol 1, ASIN:** Vol 2

**The True Stories Series** is a series of books which include true stories by The Prophet of Life.

**True Stories!**
A riveting collection of true stories. Whether you want to know about the toddler taken by a gator at a Disney Resort, an 18 year old who doesn't exist, which popular restaurant chain has a corporate mentality of public humiliation for its employees or an alarming new trend that could affect your household this book has got it all and they are all absolutely true!
**Author:** The Prophet of Life   **ISBN: 978-1-936462-16-2**
**ASIN: B06XVSZSZ9**

**True Stories: Inspiration and General Interest**
**SP**
What do cell phone addicts, George Orwell, birds, Paul McCartney, The Nobel Prize, Black Friday, Led Zeppelin, garbage, a pep talk, tipping, Steve Jobs, Shakespeare, inspirational thoughts and your mother have in common? They are in true stories in this book. True Stories of Inspiration & General Interest brings together stories and poems about celebrities, trends and everyday people. Sometimes surprising, always interesting, it will entertain you and give you something to think about at the same time.

**Author:** The Prophet of Life   **ISBN: 978-1-936462-15-5 ASIN: B00TXWVNUC   ASIN: B01BBCKFZU (Spanish Edition)**

**Controversy**

**SP**

What do Caitlyn Jenner, Donald Trump, a cure for AIDS, Chinese hackers, Adolf Hitler and Global Warming have in common? They are all at the heart of a controversy and there are stories about them in this unique book that turns tabloid headlines inside out.

**Author:** The Prophet of Life   **ISBN:  978-1-936462-19-3 ASIN: B016MWU8NS   ASIN:  B01CRF3098 (Spanish Edition)**

**True Stories of Crime and Punishment**
**SP**

This book of serious crime stories is ripped from headlines all over the globe. From the family that vanished, to the 11 year old girl killed in a fight over a boy, to the prisoner who hasn't eaten in 14 years, to the severed human head found near the famous Hollywood sign these stories ripped will astound you and give you pause to think.

**Author:** The Prophet of Life  **ISBN: 978-1-936462-17-9 ASIN: B01406YZBE  ASIN:  B01N10ND7S (Spanish Edition)**

**Strange but True!**

A collection of facts and stories about people, places and things that are strange and seem like fiction but are absolutely true!

**Author:** Mark Wilkins **ISBN: ASIN:**

**The A Storyteller Series** is a unique book series. Instead of concentrating on a particular character or genre, the series consists of collections of short stories by Author Mark Wilkins, Also Known As A Storyteller.

**Slices of Life Volume 1**
                    **SP**
is a collection of humorous short stories about life. Most of them deal with marriage and family members. From smart spouses to intelligent little children to guys trying to impress their friends and in-laws trying to master technology each story is like a little slice of life but together, they make up an irresistible pie. Sit back, grab a cup of coffee and enjoy some slices of lie because, before you know it, you will have finished the whole thing.
**Author:** Mark Wilkins **ISBN: 978-1-936462-11-7**
**ASIN: B014ZF5VY0    ASIN:  B01BBBZUL0 (Spanish Edition)**

**Slices of Life Volume 2**
                    **SP**

This sequel to Slices of Life has more humorous stories about the rich, the poor and the middle class. It even has a story about one of their pets. Ignorance is the main theme of this book, ignorance that has consequences that are sometimes touching but always humorous. So brew so coffee or tea, sit down and relax and enjoy another satisfying batch of more slice of life because, before you know it, you will have devoured the whole thing.
**Author:** Mark Wilkins **ISBN: 978-1-936462-12-4**
**ASIN: B01M2B3YZ1  ASIN:** B06XKP5C66
**(Spanish Edition)**


**Stories of The Supernatural Volume 1**
**SP**
Ghosts, demonic creatures, and Death. This collection of Short Stories will haunt and entertain you. Whether it's the classic evil of A Lump of Coal or the whimsy of A Ghost in the House this collection of Short Stories and poems will haunt, thrill and entertain you.
**Author:** Mark Wilkins **ISBN:** 978-1-936462-18-6
**ASIN:** B01M1N1QR5   **ASIN:** B01MA12YXY
**(Spanish Edition)**

**Stories of The Supernatural Volume 2**
**SP**

In this sequel to Stories of The Supernatural there are more Ghosts, Demonic Creatures and Death. This collection of short stories Centers of Ghosts and Monsters. Within its pages you will marvel at the exploits of The Soul Collector, Shudder at the mention of the dreaded Bungadun and of the Hell Banger and ride the rails on the ghost train. Strap on your seat belts, it's going to be a bumpy ride! **Author:** Mark Wilkins **ISBN:** 978-1-936462-26-1 **ASIN:** B01MDJMSUY        **ASIN:** B01M4FXDL1     **(Spanish Edition)**

**A Week's Worth of Fiction:** Volume 1
SP

7 unusual stories of fiction that explores different sides of the genre. From what is going through the mind of a suicide bomber to a teacher on the edge sanity to an everyman who becomes a hero through senseless violence a journey of dark adventures awaits you.

**Author:** Mark Wilkins     **ISBN: 978-1-936462-13-1 ASIN: B01521SQ02    ASIN:        B06XVD21PM (Spanish Edition)**

## A Week's Worth of Fiction Volume 2
### SP

From a girl battling a corporation over the rights to her blood to people engaging in life and death struggles this sequel to A Week's Worth of Fiction gives you 7 more stories that will thrill you, surprise you and make you think. Often dystopic and sometimes surreal, if you want stories you will never forget you only need to count to 7.

**Author:** Mark Wilkins  **ISBN:** 978-1-936462-14-8 **ASIN:** B01LX9RZH7  **ASIN:** B071GCYFK6 **(Spanish Edition)**

## A Week's Worth of Fiction Volume 3
### SP

From a woman trying to find love before her looks fade to a sky marshal struggling with racism to how Karma affects the life of a sanitation worker, this sequel to A Week's Worth of Fiction gives you 7 more stories that will thrill you, surprise you and make you think. Often dystopic and sometimes surreal, if you want stories you will never forget you only need to count to 7.

**Author:** Mark Wilkins  **ASIN:**     B071WNC6ZX
     **ASIN:  B072K6J9HN    (Spanish Edition)**

## A Week's Worth of Fiction Volume 4
### SP

From a soldier trying to solve a mystery to an indigenous man fighting barbaric tribal customs to a study of good and evil with a surprise outcome this sequel to A Week's Worth of Fiction gives you 7 more stories that will thrill you, surprise you and make you think. Often dystopic and sometimes surreal, if you want stories you will never forget you only need to count to 7.

**Author:** Mark Wilkins                **ASIN:**
**B07217QL6H    ASIN:  B071JVQQ96    (Spanish Edition)**

**Classroom Confessions** Volume 1
       **SP**
is a series of true stories from the front lines of public
education. Within its pages you will meet quirky
characters, the good, the bad and the over
caffeinated. Some of them are teachers, some
students and some are administrators. Some will
make you laugh, others will make you cry but they
all play an important role in public education. Their
stories are written in way that will entertain you and
give you something to think about.
**Author:** Mark Wilkins  **ISBN: 978-1-936462-08-7**
**ASIN: B00VNFJBX8    ASIN:  B01MSV4N92**
**(Spanish Edition)**

**Classroom Confessions Volume 2**
       **SP**

Is another series of true stories from the front lines of
public education. Within its pages you will meet
unforgettable characters like the French Substitute,
Mr. Happyhands, Harry Winkwater, The
Bushwhacker and of course, Julian. Some will touch
your heart, others will give you something to think
about but they will all entertain you. **Author:** Mark
Wilkins    **ASIN: B01N1OCRVC  ASIN:**
**B06XC9HDQV (Spanish Edition)**

**The Love Force Novella Series:** These are short novels of varying length.

Karma: The story of one man who negotiates between two different cultures, and opposing life views competing for his attention. His conflicts and struggles are overshadowed by cosmic forces he cannot understand. Karma provides insights into the struggles and conflicts we all face. **Author: Mark Wilkins**

**ASIN: B0722R448R  (English Edition)  ASIN: B072Z6L36V      (Spanish Edition)**

**Coming Soon!!!!! Love Force International Paperbacks! Paperback duos (2 books in 1) and Trilogies (3 books in 1).**

**The Beyond Faith Series**

Is a series of books that look at life from a spiritual perspective. No matter what your faith, you will find spiritual insights in these books that will enrich your life.

**What Faith Has Taught Me**
**SP**
 I am just an ordinary person who has been privileged to have a life filled with miracles and revelations. There are many times when I had nothing except faith but faith was all I needed to sustain me. My faith and my God have taught me many life lessons.  This book shares some of the things my faith has taught me and the spiritual insights I have gained because of my faith.
**Author:** The Prophet of Life   **ISBN:  978-1-936462-03-2   ASIN: B01527IKT8   ASIN:  B01EE3QSW2 (Spanish Edition)**

**Finding God in A Chaotic World**

The world can seem so chaotic these days. Many
people long for guidance. Many others want to get
closer to God. How do you find God amidst the
chaos and confusion? How can you discern God's
messages from the multi-media blitz we are each
bombarded with every day? Some people are part of
an organized religion. Others are spiritual without a
particular religion. Some are still searching, All of
them trying to find God.

In this book, you will learn that The Lord
communicates with how The Lord communicates
with you. You will learn about the True Nature of
God and realize just how profound God's Love and
reach are. You will learn the secret of why God's will
always prevails. If you are ready for revelations that
may change the way you look at life in general and
your life in particular, read this book.

**Author:** The Prophet of Life **ISBN: 978-1-936462-01-8
ASIN: B00SLLZAAU**

**Finding God without Religion**

People of faith are not exclusive to religion. There are many who are spiritual or agnostic. They don't fit into the doctrine, rituals and congregational community of religion. In this wisdom filled volume, people of faith but without an organized religion can gain insights into life, the afterlife and God without being brow beaten or guilt tripped into conversion. This volume is Book 2 of the Revelations of 2012 Beyond Faith series. Part 1 is entitled Finding God in A Chaotic World.
**Author:** The Prophet of Life  **ISBN: 978-1-936462-10-0**
**ASIN: B00XKPD86K**

**Inspiration For All 1**
            **SP**
Selected Inspirational Writings. Whether you are of faith or just in need of inspiration in your life, this book full of inspirational stories, poems and essays will sustain and strengthen you on your journey.
**Authors: The Prophet of Life & Mark Wilkins**
**ASIN: B071ZM17V6**

**Inspiration for All 2**
            **SP**
This is a book of selected inspirational writings by three different authors. It will not only entertain you but will also stimulate your mind by offering you alternative ways of looking at things and opportunities to gain insights. **Authors**: Mark Wilkins, The Prophet of Life & Dr. Goose. **ASIN: B0736JH6M9**  Spanish **ASIN:  B072WK9JBH**

**Outrageous Humor Series**
Books of stories and fake news articles for those with
an off-beat sense of humor.

**Outrageous Stories**
This book is filled with offbeat humor articles. All of
them are fictitious and many of them completely
outrageous. No one is safe from being made fun of be
they terrorists, Presidents, Dictators, The Movie and
Record Business or couch potatoes. If you are college
age or older and have an offbeat, irreverent, sense of
humor, this book is for you!
**Author:** Mark Wilkins **ISBN: 978-1-936462-33-9**
**ASIN:** B01LY3VZJR

**More Outrageous Stories**
This book is filled with more offbeat humor articles.
All of them are fictitious and many of them
completely outrageous. No one is safe from being
made fun of be they terrorists, Racists, National
Holidays or the medical establishment. If you are
college age or older and have an offbeat, irreverent,
sense of humor, this book is for you!
**Author:** Mark Wilkins **ISBN: 978-1-936462-33-9**
**ASIN:**

**Self Help Series**
This consists of books by different authors designed
to help people improve their lives.

**Becoming The Person You've Always Wanted to Be SP**
This self-help book offers a simple, yet profound method of making positive changes in your life. It includes a link to download exclusive, helpful companion worksheets to help you become the person you have always wanted to be.
**Author:** Mark Wilkins **ISBN: 978-1-936462-39-1**
ASIN:                     **ASIN: B01MSYVU6R (Spanish Edition)**

**Life Success Kit**
Spiritual Thought Leader The Prophet of Life helps you clarify what success really means to you through a series of inspirational life lessons designed to give you new perspectives on achieving success and a blueprint for making changes in the things that are preventing you from becoming a success.
**Author:** The Prophet of Life          **ASIN:** B01MZ2TSCP

**The Your Life in Rhyme Poetry Series**
Is a series of Poetry books unlike any you have ever
read whether it is an exploration of life itself through
a thematic chapter on each of the various stages of
life as in Reflections in The Mirror of Life, The
mixture of thought provoking essays and
inspirational poetry of Black in America or the
exploration of a single topic as in Romance Returns
or Life in Verse. The books in this series will have
you rediscovering poetry in a way that will make you
wonder why you ever avoided it in the first place.

**Reflections in the Mirror of Life** This unique book
explores life through its harsh realities, pleasant
diversions and positive possibilities. The book looks
at modern society, the problems it faces, and the
people who are a part of it. In a unique twist that's
different from most books of poetry, Reflections is
divided into five chapters, each of which explores a
different theme woven into the fabric of modern life.
The tone for each chapter is set by a free verse poem
which is followed by a series of rhyming poems on
that theme.
**Author:** The Prophet of Life **ISBN: 978-1-936462-04-9**
**ASIN: B00V2TSAXC**

**Black in America** is an exploration of racism through essays and poems. It spans from the beginnings of the Civil Rights movement through today. It looks at people who have been lightning rods for race relations in America and has some surprising insights into the people and events that have shaped race relations in America for the past 60 years. This book is a good companion for anyone who wants to gain insight into the Civil Rights movement, race relations and racism itself.   **Author:** The Prophet of Life   **ISBN:** 978-1-936462-09-4
ASIN: B00S05QSXA

**Every Lyric Tells A Story**   A collection of unique song lyrics that tell compelling stories about people, their lives, their hopes and dreams. You can find yourself and people you know in many of them.
**Author:** The Prophet of Life & Mark Wilkins   **ISBN:**
**ASIN:** B01NAFDWZW

**Romance Lives** A Collections of romantic love poems. It is divided into three sections. The Hunger about the need for love we all have, the romance about courtship ritual of romancing it takes to create a lasting in the one you choose and the deep emotions involved in making love a lasting love.
**Author: The Prophet of Life  ISBN:    ASIN:**

**Life in Verse**

A collection of poems about life. The poems and song lyrics are about people, their lives, their hopes and dreams. You can find yourself and people you know in many of them. **Author:** The Prophet of Life **ISBN:** **ASIN:**

**The Best Quotes quotation series**
Is a series of books filled with quotes attributed to the Prophet of Life whose quotes have been used by charities, corporations, institutions of Medicine and higher learning. The book includes a license to use any of the quotes as long as they are attributed to The Prophet of Life.

**The Best Quotes About God**
**SP**
This short book is filled with some of the more popular quotes about God attributed to The Prophet of Life. It is both thought provoking and inspirational. It is filled with dozens of quotes about God that one can read and copy for personal use.

**Author:** The Prophet of Life **ISBN: 978-1-936462-20-9**
**ASIN: B018P0M8OC  ASIN:  B01BJXYHLY**
**(Spanish Edition)**

## The Best Quotes on General Subjects

This short book is filled with some of the more popular quotes on general subjects attributed to The Prophet of Life. The book includes quotes on topics such as life, love, happiness, crime and punishment, wellness and includes many of the humorous quotes attributed to The Prophet of Life. You will find the wit and wisdom in its pages thought provoking and inspirational. It is filled with dozens of quotes about God that one can read and copy for personal use.

**Author:**  The Prophet of Life  **ISBN:**    **ASIN:**
**B01M58L9LW**

## The Best Spiritual Quotes

This book is filled with some of the more popular quotes on Spiritual Subjects attributed to The Prophet of Life. Included are quotes on faith, mercy, life lessons, humanity and spirituality. You should find them to be profound, thought provoking and inspirational. It is filled with many pages of quotes that one can read and copy for personal use.

**Author:** The Prophet of Life    **ASIN:**
**B01MQVA87Q**

**Children Storybook Series**
All books are by Dr. Goose who writes in both prose
and rhyming verse.

**Classic Children's Stories You've Likely Never
Heard  SP**
Help develop your child's creative abilities and
develop their imagination by reading them stories
from this book that has no illustrations. Whether it's
a story about Prince trying to find the answer to a
question, a spider talking about a savior, a kingdom
in trouble or a child trying to save the world you will
find yourself wanting to read these children's stories
with international flavor again and again. This first
book in the series is for smaller children.
**Author:** Dr. Goose **ISBN:** 978-1-936462-40-7 **ASIN:**
B01NAF8QNU            **ASIN:** B01MR5PR84
**(Spanish Edition)**

**More Classic Children's Stories You've Likely
Never Heard   SP**

This sequel gives you more unknown classics. The book introduces new characters like a little chicken whose life is similar to a person's and a ballad about a hairy man. There is a story about a prince whose refusal causes an international incident. There is even an updated version of classic children's story everyone knows from different character's points of view. This second book in the series helps tweens and juvenile children creative abilities and develop their imagination as stories from this book that has no illustrations either.
**Author:** Dr. Goose **ISBN:** 978-1-936462-41-4 **ASIN:**
                **ASIN:**      **(Spanish Edition)**

**My First Book of Stupid Little Fables**                        **SP**
Whether the greed of mooches and lunch thieves, sadistic children, or bizarre stories about pets this first installment in the series of irreverently humorous stories with twisted endings about the selfish and the greedy delivers. It even has the stupid little drawings!  For Juveniles.
**Author:** Dr. Goose    **ISBN: 978-1-936462-44-5  ASIN:**
                **ASIN:**      **(Spanish Edition)**

**My Second Book of Stupid Little Fables**
**SP**

Whether it's well-meaning but incompetent grandmas, egotistical women, sadistic children, or crazy people in shopping centers, this second installment in the series of irreverently humorous stories with twisted endings about the selfish and the greedy delivers. It even has the drawings you love to make fun of just like the first one!   For Juveniles.
**Author:** Dr. Goose      **ISBN:**      **ASIN:**
     **ASIN:**        **(Spanish Edition)**

More Children's Stories
School Kidz Volume 1 Elementary and Middle
School   SP
Six funny stories about kids who are smarter than
their age. Within its pages you will meet A boy
whose vocabulary is better than the adults in his
school, a kid who escapes a spanking, A kid who gets
a new cell phone with a built in problem and a
brother and sister who learn how get rid of junk from
an old aunt. Recommended for kidz ages 12-16.
**Author: Mark Wilkins ASIN:**  B0717B6SQ4

**School Kidz Volume 2 High School**          **SP**
9 stories about kids who are in high school. Within its
pages you will meet a group of Kidz who get
involved in a rotten egg war, a girl who doesn't exist,
and a kid who sends a friend on a date with his
sister. Recommended for kidz ages 14-18. **Author:
Mark Wilkins ASIN:** B071W5WZZN

# Coming Soon E Workbooks and an E Textbook!
# A series of mini and one comprehensive E Textbook Under the title of Mr. Wilkins Teaches English by Mark Wilkins

The specific mini textbooks will be on topics such as Reading and Responding to Literature, and Methods for Writing Paragraphs and Essays. The Comprehensive text will include a weekly spelling component and both the mini texts and comprehensive Text will include creative lessons that promote creativity and critical thinking in students while fitting into common core standards. The mini texts will be no more than 99 cents each and the comprehensive text will be paperback for under $10! All of the books are freshly created and contain exclusive intellectual property you won't find in any other texts. These books are perfect for students learning high school English levels 9 & 10 whether you are a classroom teacher or are home schooling your child. We are making the commitment to keep all of the books at low prices to allow parents and school districts to afford texts in the face of shrinking educational budgets. Purchasers will be given an opportunity to receive an email with a printable version of the exercises and assignments as well as links to online testing free of charge.

**Author:** Mark Wilkins     **ISBN:**     **ASIN:**

## Compelling Stories for Adaptation to Short Film
### For Film Students

Compelling stories in a set location with six or less characters. Easily adaptable to screenplay with notes on adapting them.

**Author:** Mark Wilkins     **ISBN:**     **ASIN:**